FIRST LOVE

Renewing Your Passion for God

BILL BRIGHT

NewLife
PUBLICATIONS

First Love: Restoring Your Passion for God

Published by
New*Life* Publications
A ministry of Campus Crusade for Christ
P.O. Box 620877
Orlando, FL 32862-0877

Design and production by Genesis Group

Cover design by Koechel Peterson & Associates, Inc., Minneapolis, MN

Printed in the United States of America

ISBN 1-56399-188-8

Unless otherwise indicated, Scripture quotations are from the *New Living Translation*, © 1996 by Tyndale House Publishers, Inc., Wheaton, Illinois.

Scripture quotations designated NIV are from the *New International Version*, © 1973, 1978, 1984 by the International Bible Society. Published by Zondervan Bible Publishers, Grand Rapids, Michigan.

CONTENTS

ACKNOWLEDGMENTS

I ESPECIALLY WANT to thank Rob Suggs and Jim Bramlett, whose help with research and writing was invaluable to the creation of this book. I am very appreciative of Brenda Josee for her conceptual insights and editing, and Lynn Copeland of Genesis Group for the final edit. I am grateful to Helmut Teichert for his oversight of this project, and also want to thank the other team members for their significant contributions: John Barber, theological review; John Nill, publisher; Tammy Campbell, editorial assistant; and Michelle Treiber, cover coordinator and print broker.

There is one person more than any other who deserves special recognition: my beloved bride of over fifty years, Vonette. We have experienced many years of God's abundant love and blessing.

FOREWORD

FOR MOST OF MY LIFE, I have admired Bill Bright as a champion for world evangelism and Spirit-filled living. Not until I read his new book, *First Love*, did I understand completely the spiritual dynamic that has driven him for the fifty years of his ministry.

As I read the pages of *First Love*, I realized that the highest priority in Dr. Bright's life has not been Campus Crusade, or even evangelism. His first priority has been, and is today, his personal relationship with the Lord Jesus Christ.

As I read his testimony in the early pages of this book, I was moved to tears as he described his deep love for the Lord. From his early experience as a Christian businessman, to his position of great influence in the world, Bill Bright has had one passion: to know the Lord and to love Him deeply.

But this book is much more than the account of Bill Bright's spiritual journey. It is a carefully drawn roadmap for all of us who desire an intimate walk with the Lord.

From the words of Jesus Christ to the Ephesian church, recorded in Revelation chapter two, Dr. Bright reviews the spiritual formula for returning to a "first love" relationship with the Lord. The steps he has identifed provide the focus for this powerful challenge to the hungry believer's heart. The discussion on the subject of prayer and fasting alone is worth the price of the book.

I measure the impact of a book by what it causes me to think and do as the result of having read it. As I write this foreword, it is the end of the calendar year. During this time, I have always tried to spend extra time reviewing the past year and preparing my heart for the year to come. More than anything else, *First Love* has occupied my heart and mind during these days as I have reviewed the impact of Dr. Bright's life.

This book has caused me to want to cultivate an even deeper relationship with the Lord and has reminded me that no matter what we may accomplish in our work for the Lord, it is our walk with the Lord that matters most.

It will take you only a few moments to read this book; but if you read it prayerfully, it just might change the rest of your life.

DR. DAVID JEREMIAH
Senior Pastor,
Shadow Mountain Community Church
President, Turning Point Ministries

"Write this letter to the angel of the church in Ephesus. This is the message from the one who holds the seven stars in his right hand, the one who walks among the seven gold lampstands: 'I know all the things you do. I have seen your hard work and your patient endurance. I know you don't tolerate evil people. You have examined the claims of those who say they are apostles but are not. You have discovered they are liars. You have patiently suffered for me without quitting.

"'But I have this complaint against you. You don't love me or each other as you did at first! Look how far you have fallen from your first love! Turn back to me again and work as you did at first. If you don't, I will come and remove your lampstand from its place among the churches. But there is this about you that is good: You hate the deeds of the immoral Nicolaitans, just as I do. Anyone who is willing to hear should listen to the Spirit and understand what the Spirit is saying to the churches. Everyone who is victorious will eat from the tree of life in the paradise of God.'"

REVELATION 2:1–7

INTRODUCTION

THE GREATEST POWER known to man is love. In 1 Corinthians 13, Paul explains how important love is to God: "If I could speak in any language in heaven or on earth but didn't love others, I would only be making meaningless noise like a loud gong or a clanging cymbal. If I had the gift of prophecy, and if I knew all the mysteries of the future and knew everything about everything, but didn't love others, what good would I be? And if I had the gift of faith so that I could speak to a mountain and make it move, without love I would be no good to anybody. If I gave everything I have to the poor and even sacrificed my body, I could boast about it; but if I didn't love others, I would be of no value whatsoever."

The Bible declares that "God is love" (1 John 4:16). Jesus of Nazareth, God in the flesh (John 1:1), was and is the personification of love—love incarnate.

While He walked on earth, Jesus always did the perfect will of God. So obeying the greatest of all the commandments—"You must love the Lord your God with all your heart, all your soul, all your mind, and all your strength" and "Love your neighbor as yourself"—was no challenge for Him. However, it is a daily challenge for us. How do we obey this greatest commandment so that we never leave our "first love" for God? By relying on our risen Lord.

According to God's Word, the Christian life is not what we do for Christ but what He does in and through us (Galatians 2:20). So if Christ, the distilled essence of love, lives in and through us as we are surrendered to His will and empowered by His Spirit, loving becomes His responsibility.

This book explains how we can return to and maintain our "first love" for God. Its simple biblical truths will guarantee the most exciting adventure the human spirit can ever know. Before you read any further, I invite you to pray the following prayer:

"Dear Lord, as I read these pages, please help me to understand and experience afresh your unconditional love for me and show me how to return to my first love for You."

one

WANDERING, NOT LOST

Whether we are high above the sky or in the deepest ocean, nothing in all creation will ever be able to separate us from the love of God that is revealed in Christ Jesus our Lord.

ROMANS 8:39

THE LIFE STORY of Robert Robinson is one of the most moving that I have ever read. It gives heartwarming insights into God's ability to turn tragedy into triumph. Robinson reminds me of so many men and women I have known through the years. Perhaps you will recognize something of yourself in his experience.

Robinson wrote the unforgettable words to the hymn *Come Thou Fount of Every Blessing*, one of my favorites. He was a good man who became a Christian when he was 17, through the influence of the great preacher George Whitefield. He later entered the ministry to serve Christ with great love and devotion.

But Robinson was an honest man, too, and he acknowledged a difficult truth about himself. His love for Jesus was deep but not dependable. At times his passion for God waned, and the well of his devotion ran dry. Sometimes he felt nothing at all for His Lord. His heart was prone to wander.

This cold truth troubled Robinson. He grappled with it, began to write out his thoughts and feelings, and finally produced a timeless hymn. *Come Thou Fount* is an autobiographical story of a man so unworthy, so unfaithful, yet always forgiven to come home to the loving arms of his Lord.

As time moved on and Robinson grew older, he wandered farther and farther from God. His actions and attitudes began to darken, and he came to feel that the distance between God and himself had become too great to be reconciled. Sin and corruption had taken root in his life. How could he ever look into the eyes of Jesus again? Robert Robinson was a miserable man, consumed by the grief of his own guilt. With the restless heart of Jonah, of the Prodigal Son, and of every guilt-ridden soul, he took to the road. Perhaps some distant land would hold the cure. Perhaps he could somehow leave his self-condemnation behind.

One day, in the midst of his journeys, a young lady was seated across from him in a stagecoach.

She was filled with the joy of Christ and could talk of nothing else. Robinson, of course, would have chosen any other topic available. But he was a captive audience; he could not, obviously, leap out of a moving carriage. So he resigned himself to a discussion of spiritual matters. In those days, people used hymnals as devotional books, and this young lady had such a volume in her lap. She said, "Sir, I'd like your opinion of one of these hymns—one that has been such a powerful influence in my life." And she handed the hymnal across to him.

Robinson looked at the page and found himself confronted by his own words. His throat ran dry and he could think of nothing to say. He tried to hand the book back to her. But the young lady persisted, assuming he must be as moved by the words to *Come Thou Fount* as she was. Maybe that was the reason for the sudden wetness in his eyes, the great tears sliding down his face. But slowly the realization dawned on her that she was looking into the countenance of a tortured soul.

Robinson saw that she knew the truth. He began to nod slowly, then the words finally followed: "I am the man who wrote that hymn," he said. "Many years ago. I'd give anything to experience that joy again—*anything*."

The woman was shocked. She looked down at the page and saw the name of the poet who was sitting across from her: *Robert Robinson*. His life story was written in the ink below her, and his portrait was painted in the tears of the man before her.

The young lady pointed to the lines he knew so well. She began to speak gently about the "streams of mercy, never ceasing" that were still deep enough to drown his tears. She showed him there were no seasons too lengthy, no distance too great for the love of God to find him, comfort him, and bring him home again.

Holding On for Dear Life

That day Robert Robinson, broken and defeated, rediscovered the love he had left behind. I can imagine the joy he felt, because in my own life, that first love is everything.

Quite often people ask me, "How can I pray for you?" I always answer them the same way. I want them to pray that wherever I go and whatever I do, I will never leave my first love. Ever since I was a young Christian, astounded by the power of God's presence and overwhelmed with His love, I have made it my first priority to hold on for dear life to my intimate, personal relationship with Him. Through my more than fifty busy years with my Lord, there have been countless problems, challenges, and opportunities. I knew in the very beginning that simply serving God was not enough. I longed to possess a heart overflowing with love and praise for my Lord. If I failed to maintain my first love, my disobedience would undermine all I hold dear. I knew that in time I would disintegrate as a believer, as a husband, a father, a person, and a businessman. My first love for God—Father, Son, and Holy Spirit—is everything to me.

Simply serving God was not enough. I longed to possess a heart overflowing with love and praise for my Lord.

For me, the price of maintaining that devotion has been daily submission. As partners in marriage, Vonette and I, as a practice, begin each morning and end each evening on our knees in prayer, acknowledging the Lord Jesus as our Master, Savior, and King. The Bible teaches that the living Christ dwells in every believer. In different words, we ask Him each day to walk around in our bodies, think with our minds, love with our hearts, speak with our lips, and continue "seeking and saving" the lost through our efforts. All day long, I seek to walk and talk with my Savior no matter what the business of the day might be. If I can cling to His love from one moment to the next, I know I will never leave it. In this way I seek to "pray continually" (1 Thessalonians 5:17, NIV) as I "practice the presence of God" (Brother Lawrence, *Practicing the Presence of God*).

In these recent times I have faced new medical challenges: incurable fibrosis of the lungs, cancer, and diabetes. When I pour out my prayers to God and read His Word, I can no longer fall to my knees quite so easily. If I did, the Lord knows I would have trouble rising again. But He understands that. He cares more about a sturdy heart than wobbly knees.

I see doctors regularly and have had my share of surgeries. I now depend upon the help of a wonderful apparatus almost 24 hours each day to help me breath the oxygen I need. As Job once said, "The LORD gave me everything I had, and the LORD has taken it away. Praise the name of the LORD!" (Job 1:21). Yes, He has given me so much, all through the years and right up to the present. But the greatest gift of all, in those wonderful

16

words that Robert Robinson gave us, is a heart that can be tuned to sing his praise. Much of my mobility has been taken away. I have lost over half of my breathing capacity and much of the energy to do all that I would like to do for Him. At age 80, I have far fewer days before me than I have behind me. But God has left me with the one thing that I treasure most: the ability to love Him with my first love, and to praise Him with my mind and emotions every moment that I live on this earth. By the grace of God, I will never take leave of my first love for Him.

We're Inseparable

Not that my heart is as pure as I would like it to be—I do not want to give you the impression that I am perfect. No one is perfect but Jesus. I have the same traces of sin and rebellion within me that all of us must confront. Daily my flesh wars against my spirit (Galatians 5:16,17). My heart is prone to wander just as yours is. It requires daily vigilance to protect my spirit from leaving my first love. But it is more than worth the struggle and daily discipline. God's love is so strengthening and so refreshing. I can face any medical problem that may lie before me. I can face the prospect of death itself with joy. But I could never face the possibility of separation from that perfect love of God that sustains my spirit. I take great comfort from God's wonderful assurance recorded in Romans 8:38,39:

> *I am convinced that nothing can ever separate us from his love. Death can't, and life can't. The angels can't, and the demons can't. Our fears for today, our worries about tomorrow, and even the powers of hell can't keep God's love away. Whether we are high above the sky or in the deepest ocean, nothing in all creation will ever be able to separate us from the love of God that is revealed in Christ Jesus our Lord.*

So you see, there is absolutely nothing that can separate you or me from that first love. Not even the angels and demons can come between God and us. Not even death itself can provide a barrier. The only thing that can take away my first love is my own spirit, prone to wander.

First Corinthians 13:13 tells us of "three things that will endure—faith, hope, and love—and the greatest of these is love." My faith will be fulfilled one day, when I see Jesus face to face. All my hopes will be complete. But my love for God, and

His love for me, will endure forever, from now right into eternity. The Bible says it is the greatest thing of all. I would not want to leave that even for an instant.

What about you? Has your spirit somehow moved away from the wonderful love of God? How would you describe the state of your affection for Him today? Can you remember how it felt on the day you first met Him? How far have you wandered from the place where He wants you to be? What will it take for you to return to that first love that He wants each of us to experience as a way of life?

Those are some of the questions I pray we can answer in this book.

Jesus commanded us to love God with all our heart, soul, mind, and strength. I do not believe there is any issue more crucial for you and me to consider in this life. As Paul has shown us, there is no distance of time or space that can keep you from His wonderful love. You may run halfway around the world, and you may hide from God for the best years of your life. No matter what your circumstances, what you may have done, or how long you may have rebelled, God's heart of love remains open to you. You *can* go home again—home to the arms of the Father who will never stop waiting for you with His love, never stop seeking to restore the joy and wonder of your salvation.

Take and Seal It

If, as a believer, your heart is prone to wander; if your well of devotion has run dry; if you have somehow, through the busyness of life and the maze of challenges and relationships, left your first love—this book is for you, my friend. If you do not know our Lord Jesus Christ personally, my prayer is that this book will help you make the most wonderful discovery possible for time and eternity. Then, when your heart is united with the heart of God, be sure to bind them together for the glory of God and your eternal blessing. Mr. Robinson's song put it so beautifully:

> *Prone to wander, Lord, I feel it.*
> *Prone to leave the God I love.*
> *Here's my heart, Lord, take and seal it.*
> *Seal it for Thy courts above.*

Through the years I have learned a lot about surgery, but that verse describes an operation I recommend for each of us: the sealing of our hearts to the great, loving heart of God. Would you like to have that happen in your life? Would you like to know that you are in the presence of a wonderful, loving Father once and for all, inseparable forever?

It will happen, if you truly want it to. Today you can discover how the Lord can seal your heart. You will have the marvelous assurance that His wonderful, all-surpassing, unconditional love will never let you go—and from that moment on, you will never let *Him* go.

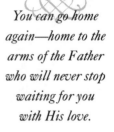

You can go home again—home to the arms of the Father who will never stop waiting for you with His love.

Your first love will become your ultimate and final one, and the love of all your days, hours, and moments for all time and eternity.

TRANSFORMED BY LOVE

*This is real love. It is not that we loved
God, but that he loved us and sent his Son
as a sacrifice to take away our sins.*
1 JOHN 4:10

THE LOVE OF GOD took me entirely by surprise.
It was the last thing that I expected, and the only
thing that could have completely captured my
devotion.

In 1945, I was a young businessman in Hollywood with the whole world before me. I was
working long hours, chasing the American dream
of building my own business and a financial fortune. Frankly, I was off to a very promising start.
Business was going well. But from my first day in
California, something unexpected and unusual began to happen to me—something that can only be
accounted for by the sovereign, invisible, loving
hand of God.

I had just arrived in Los Angeles and was on
my way to Pasadena. I happened to pick up a
hitchhiker by the side of the road. I should men-

tion that I do not recommend hitchhiking or pick-ing up riders in today's dangerous times, but no one considered it risky half a century ago. It was simply an act of kindness. This particular hitch-hiker was a friendly young man who kindly invit-ed me to spend the night in the home of Dawson and Lila Trotman. Dawson was the founder of the great Christian movement The Navigators, of which my passenger was a member. Later that evening, I was invited to the home of Charles E. Fuller for a birthday party for his son Dan (many years later I was privileged to be the best man in Dan and Ruth's wedding). Can you imagine—here I was, an unbeliever, spending my first night in Los Angeles in the homes of two of the greatest Christian leaders of the twentieth century! How can one explain such a remarkable experience? In retrospect, my saintly mother was praying that God would watch over me and direct my steps. He was simply answering her prayer.

Over a year passed and I was invited to visit one of the city's finest churches, the First Pres-byterian Church of Hollywood. It had a vibrant young adult group that immediately attracted me. As I attended their meetings and classes, I was amazed at what I observed among the members.

They had a special quality about them—a dynamic, positive charisma that I had never seen in such abundance. Church had not meant much to me before this time, but these people had an infectious spirit about them. I became more and more involved with the group until I was forced, over a period of months, to confront my own spiritual condition.

It was as if Jesus stepped right out of that Holy Book and commanded my full and complete devotion.

I looked for my old, neglected Bible, which my mother had given me when I was a young teenager. Wiping off the dust, I began to study the life and words of Jesus with new interest. I had been raised by a godly mother; I had been to church and had heard a few sermons. But the words of the Gospels seemed brand new, as if I had never heard them before. They absorbed me and captivated my spirit. Over a period of months, as I listened to sermons and read God's Word, it was as if Jesus stepped right out of that Holy Book and commanded my full and complete devotion. I was convinced that He was the most incredible and remarkable person to ever walk this earth.

My teacher at church, Dr. Henrietta Mears, was another "chance" acquaintance whom God sent to me at this crucial time. Her passion for Jesus not only influenced my life, but lead to the founding of a publishing house, a conference retreat center, Bible study materials still in use today, and a legacy of hundreds of men and women all over the world—including Billy Graham—whose faiths were ignited when touched by her ministry.

Dr. Mears and my pastor, Dr. Louis Evans, helped me understand that Jesus was actually much more than the greatest Man who ever lived. He was God incarnate, walking among mankind so that we could know and love Him in the fullest sense. Along with my mother, Dr. Mears and Dr. Evans showed me that Christ is Lord of all; they demonstrated the complete love and devotion a Christian ought to have for Him.

When Love Is Real

I went to California to pursue a career, but when I got there, Christ pursued me. I believe that He sovereignly put me in certain places and among specific people for His purposes. It took the right combination of events for me to finally see Jesus for who He really is. I had grown up doing my daily chores on the family ranch, listening to my mother sing hymns with quiet contentment as she worked. I had seen her rise early every day to pray and study God's Word, no matter how busy she was. But now, as a young believer, I finally understood the joy that lay beneath those melodies that filled her heart. I could finally see why she was so eager to open that leather-bound Book each morning and evening to talk with her Creator.

My father and mother had been married for 35 years in a home that was divided—he was not a believer, but he became my number one prayer target after I met Jesus. My father prayed with me and received Christ as his Savior approximately a year after He became my Lord. My parents lived for 35 more years with Christ as Lord of their marriage, a miraculous difference. Both my mother and father went to be with the Lord at age 93. We had many rich and rewarding times together.

The more I learned about Jesus, the greater my love for Him grew. First John, a letter as powerful as it is concise, taught me much about this subject of love:

> *Anyone who does not love does not know God—for God is love. God showed how much he loved us by sending his only Son into the world*

so that we might have eternal life through him.
This is real love. It is not that we loved God, but
that he loved us and sent his Son as a sacrifice to
take away our sins (1 John 4:8–10).

It is so simple! How had I missed it in the past? *God is love!* To me, those are the three most beautiful words ever written. They are the three words that turned the world upside-down, that transform all sadness into joy and all defeat into victory. No other three words could be so simple, so profound, so powerful. *God is love.*

We cannot fully appreciate the depth of that statement without considering the object of His perfect, infinite, unconditional love: *us!* Sinful, rebellious you and me. As human beings filled with disobedience, we were deserving of nothing but punishment and eternal banishment from His holy presence. Yet God Himself, deliberately as an act of His great love, endured the punishment of the cross so we could avoid it—because He is love. He submitted Himself to the most painful and degrading execution men could possibly inflict, just so He could offer His rescue from the kingdom of darkness to the very agents of His suffering. Even today, I feel deep emotion when I consider all that His death on the cross means to me.

It might have been me at the foot of that cross, pounding iron nails into His wrists. Even so, He would offer me no less love, no less forgiveness. As John put it, "This is real love." The greatest devotion we could muster can never compare.

John also says that it is not a matter of you or me trying to love God. It all begins with Him. It must, because we are incapable of loving as we should. We are only able to love Him or to love anyone else because He took the initiative; *He* first loved (1 John 4:19). He loved man from the beginning of creation and, through the long years, felt deep sorrow and anger when we continued to rebel against Him and reject His laws. Finally, moved by a love and compassion we will never understand, He personally came and rescued us once and for all at the cross.

Keep the Fire Burning

I studied the words of 1 John as a newborn Christian. I had never considered myself a "sinner," as I might have defined it as a young man back home in Coweta, Oklahoma. But now I saw things differently. Now I understood that my sins were just as terrible as those of the men who crucified my Lord. God had done so much for me, and I had done less than nothing for Him.

Money and business had been my gods. Success and fame had been my altar of worship. And yet He had loved me enough to pursue me, to place me among all these loving people, from my very first night in Southern California.

"God is love," writes John, "and all who live in love live in God, and God lives in them. And as we live in God, our love grows more perfect" (1 John 4:16,17).

Those simple words described the life for which I yearned. No longer, I decided, would I live in greed. I would, with God's help, live in love. According to this verse, that would be the proof that God lived within me. I would not stray from the love of God but strive to see it grow "more perfect." It would be reflected in my selfless devotion to God and to others.

John Calvin, the great reformer from Geneva, used the symbol of a hand holding a flaming heart. The inscription read, "My heart I give Thee, Lord, eagerly and sincerely." When I first caught fire for Christ and as my love for Him grew, some friends and I claimed that image for our own. We called ourselves the Fellowship of the Burning Heart and pledged to make ourselves totally expendable for God.

Ever since then, I have tried to keep my heart as an eternal flame of passion for God and His purposes. One Sunday afternoon in 1951, Vonette and I, after much prayer, "signed away" our lives, our future, and everything we owned or would ever own to Christ. Next to the moment of my salvation, this was the most important and liberating day of my life. We unconditionally turned over to our loving Father, our holy God and Savior, every possession, goal, or concern of our present or future. It was a contract with God to be bond-slaves to the only Master who could ever love and care for us. We were inspired to be His slaves since He had become a slave for all people (Philippians 2:7). Also Paul and Timothy in Philippians 1:1 proclaimed themselves to be slaves of Jesus, as did Peter, James, and Jude (2 Peter 1:1; James 1:1; Jude 1).

> *I have tried to keep my heart as an eternal flame of passion for God and His purposes.*

I can only say that in the more than fifty years that have followed, He has been more than faithful to keep His promises every moment of every day. Vonette and I have very few possessions. We do not even own the home in which we live or the cars we drive, but He graciously provides every need as He promised to do in Philippians 4:19.

God makes His wonderful, boundless love available to us every moment of every day. How could we live without it? How could our first love for Him ever slip away when His love is so perfect and so faithful? And yet I realize that it is a genuine danger for every Christian. Most true believers in Christ can point to a time when our hearts were on fire for Him. We loved Christ with a passion that no one could help but notice. It transformed us from the inside out. But for many reasons and without intending it, we let the flames die down until they became glowing embers. Soon there was little but a wisp of smoke and ashes. There are few things sadder than the ashes of a burned-out devotion.

Hands and Heart

Why do we let this happen? One reason may be that it is easier for many of us to be a Martha than a Mary. The story of these two sisters is found in Luke 10:38–42, and it has always fascinated me. Those who have known me well will tell you I'm a "doer" by nature; I favor action and accomplishment. I like to get things done.

I think Martha may have thought that way. Let us try to see her point of view. She lived in Bethany, not far from Jerusalem. One day Jesus came in with all of His entourage—disciples and friends—chattering, joking, arguing. With her home filled with guests, Martha fell into the role of hostess, cooking and cleaning. This was the way a first-century woman showed her devotion, and no one would have faulted her actions. It was not Martha but Mary, her sister, whose behavior might have been called into question. Mary sat right at Jesus' feet, where a true disciple would traditionally take a position. Other guests might have used chairs, but a serious disciple sat at the master's feet.

Martha, busily preparing dinner, did a very human thing. She approached Jesus and said, "Lord, doesn't it seem unfair to you that my sister just sits here while I do all the work? Tell her to come and help me" (v. 40).

To which Jesus replied with the words you and I need to hear, and to hear attentively: "My dear Martha, you are so upset over all these details! There is really only one thing worth being concerned about. Mary has discovered it—and I won't take it away from her" (vv. 41,42). Jesus knew the writing of Moses well, but He could have had the Book of Ecclesiastes in mind when He responded to Martha.

I believe Martha had a good heart but a *busy* heart. I've known the temptation to become so busy with the whirlwind of service that we take leave of the passion that first inspired that service. Soon the conflicts and challenges begin to upset and distract us, and they obviously did that to Martha. In no way is Jesus saying that we should neglect everyday responsibilities. But we cannot let those things become diversions from the "one thing worth being concerned about." As Jesus taught, we should "seek first his kingdom and his righteousness, and all these things will be given to you as well" (Matthew 6:33, NIV).

Jesus stressed this truth often. He underlined it again in the story of the sower and the seeds in Matthew 13. The farmer threw out his seeds, and they fell in various places that determined whether they took root and grew. Some of the seeds fell among thorns. After telling the story, Jesus explained that "the thorny ground represents those who hear and accept the Good News, but all too quickly the message is crowded out by the cares of this life and the lure of wealth, so no crop is produced" (Matthew 13:22).

We run in so many directions. We chase success, fame, the praise and applause of others, and so many concerns. In doing so, we forget the one thing about which we should be concerned. I believe we can avoid those thorns. We can sit at the Master's feet and listen carefully to His voice. Then our love for Him will linger. My mother had the hands of Martha and the heart of Mary. She stayed busy all day with the work of a rancher's wife and mother of seven children. But all the while, she was humming songs of worship and praise. I think she had "discovered it"—and Jesus never allowed her to lose it.

But what about you and me? What if we become busy with the details of life and leave our passion somewhere along the way?

Let us consider a group of Christians from the first century who had that experience. They fell head over heels in love with God and made a powerful impact upon a wicked city. Then somehow they left their first love.

A Love Left Behind

Near the beginning of the Book of Revelation, we

have a remarkable passage in which our Lord Jesus speaks directly to seven prominent churches of the first century. He greets each of them with a "pat on the back," a word of commendation for work well done. Then He gets down to business; He tells them what must be improved.

The first of these churches is located in the great city of Ephesus. As we read these words, it sounds as if the church had more than its share of "Marthas"—tireless servants who had busied their hands but lost their hearts.

> *I know all the things you do. I have seen your hard work and your patient endurance ... You have patiently suffered for me without quitting. But I have this complaint against you. You don't love me or each other as you did at first! Look how far you have fallen from your first love! Turn back to me again and work as you did at first. If you don't, I will come and remove your lampstand from its place among the churches (Revelation 2:2–5).*

We are going to be looking closely at these words, because they are vitally important for everyone who knows and loves God. The Lord is saying, "You have served Me well. You have suffered for Me patiently. You have endured over the long run. Good job! These are wonderful accomplishments. But I must tell you that something troubles Me deeply. I'm referring to your love for Me and for one another."

We are startled to hear these words. But He continues, "Your love is not what it once was. You have left it behind! Don't you recall how things used to be? Don't you remember the time when your hearts were ablaze with love for Me—and how that love overflowed into your relationships with each other? Oh, how you've fallen from those lofty heights! But there is good news: you can set things right again—back to how they were!"

Come home—that is the message. The original language, by the way, does not say that those believers have *lost* their first love; it says they have *left* it or *forsaken* it as an act of their will. I hope you can see what a difference that makes. We do not "lose" our love for a spouse, for a friend, or for Jesus Christ. We walk away from it. If we say we've lost something, it almost sounds as if it is just an unfortunate occurrence that is nobody's fault—something you can *lose* in the same way you would misplace your car keys. But we are responsible to take hold of the love God has poured out upon us. It is up to us to cling to it and never let it go. The Ephesians, however, had not done that. They had left their first love behind, and now God is inviting them—and us—to come home.

In the fifth verse, Jesus reveals the path that leads homeward to the place from which we should never have left. We must take these steps:

- *Remember* (2:5a)

- *Repent* (2:5b)

- *Resume* (2:5c)

The first of these, remembrance, is the work of the mind. If our hearts have grown cold, we must rely upon our minds. We may stop feeling, but we never stop thinking. So the mind is the best place to stir up the embers that will warm our hearts once again.

Remembering gives us the shock of realization—things have changed! We have loosened our hold on the greatest thing life has to offer. In remembering, we feel deep remorse that we have deliberately left home, our first love. The reflection of the mind will lead to the sorrow of the heart. When we have fully come to terms with the truth of it, only then will we be moved to repent.

We internally change our focus from ourselves toward God. Finally, we begin to do those things of first importance again.

Mind, Heart, Soul, and Strength

In its simplest terms, the path back to our first love is this:

What We Do	What We Use	What Jesus Calls It
We think. (Remember)	Mind	"Look how far..."
We feel. (Remorse)	Heart	"...you have fallen from your first love!"
We change. (Repent)	Soul	"Turn back to me again."
We work. (Resume)	Strength	"And work as you did at first."

God's plan, as we would expect, is a perfect one. It uses our mind, heart, soul, and strength—everything about us—to bring us back into His presence. He wants *all* of us, so that we may experience all of *Him*. It is no coincidence that Jesus said the greatest commandment is this: "You must love the Lord your God with *all* your heart, *all* your soul, *all* your mind, and *all* your strength"

(Mark 12:30, emphasis added).

Jesus also taught us that the second commandment followed naturally from the first one: "Love your neighbor as yourself" (v. 31). Notice that Jesus said to the Ephesians, "You don't love me *or each other* as you did at first" (Revelation 2:4, emphasis added). Love for people is the overflow that comes from a love for God. There is absolutely no way you can love the Lord with all your mind, heart, soul, and strength, and not have that love overflow into your other relationships —beginning with your nearest neighbors, your spouse and children, your parents and grandparents, aunts, uncles, and cousins. It works in both directions, too; when you lose the joy of God, you will begin to lose the joy of people.

Where are you today in that regard? Are you in a state of loving unity with the people important to you? If you're struggling with relationships in your family, in your workplace, or in your established friendships, the first place you should check is how you're getting along with God.

This is because we love God (*or* drift away from God) with every part of our being—mind, heart, soul, and strength. When Jesus spoke with His disciples in His most intimate teaching, in the Upper Room, He called it *abiding* or *remaining* in Him: "Remain in me, and I will remain in you," He tells us. "For a branch cannot produce fruit if it is severed from the vine, and you cannot be fruitful apart from me" (John 15:4).

This is the deepest meaning of maintaining your first love. As you remain in Him with every part of your being, you are as fully dependent upon Him as a branch is upon a tree or vine. If you remain, you grow more healthy and begin to bear fruit. Your relationships become richer. Your work becomes more excellent. And others come to know the Lord because they see the evidence of God in you.

This brings us to the next step. When we have reclaimed our first love for God, we experience *revival*.

In 1994 I began one of the most wonderful spiritual journeys of my life. Following our Lord's example of fasting, God led me to fast and pray for forty days for national and world revival and for the fulfillment of the Great Commission. He has led me to continue this blessed discipline each year since. After my fourth forty-day fast, God's Spirit showed me that such a fast is a vital part of the Great Commission. When He said in Matthew 28:20, "Teach these new disciples to obey all the commands I have given you," that would include the practice of fasting. No other discipline meets the conditions of 2 Chronicles 7:14 like fasting and prayer. And nothing can accelerate your return to "first love" like fasting and prayer.

This is how revivals begin, and for years I have fasted and prayed that I might live to see revival among believers within our nation and throughout the world. As a matter of fact, historical revivals and spiritual awakenings have always been marked by some signifying godly trait. I believe that when we experience the next world revival, it will be marked by a revival of *love*. This was the assurance that the Holy Spirit gave me during my first forty-day fast—that He would send a revival and it would be a revival of love.

In addressing the Ephesians, Jesus also refers to an additional event: after renewing our first love, we will receive a *reward* (Revelation 2:7). We will explore each of these steps together, and by the grace of God our devotion for Him will catch fire once again, rising to a mighty flame. Those around us will move closer, just to warm their hearts and hands in the glow of our restored first love.

three

REMEMBRANCE:
Reliving Your First Love

*Look how far you have fallen from
your first love!*
REVELATION 2:5A

I REALLY HIT THE jackpot! I found my heavenly
love and my earthly love during approximately the
same period. Even as I was making the wonderful discovery of God's goodness, He showed me
that Vonette Zachary was the right life partner for
me.

I remember sitting across the dinner table
from her the night I proposed, after taking her to
the Red Bud Ball at Texas Women's University
where she was a sophomore. I told her all about
my ambitious plans for life and how they all in-
cluded her. I was living in Hollywood, a city filled
with beautiful women. But in my eyes, none of
them could compare with the beauty of Vonette,
inside and outside. Her positive response thrilled
my heart. Together we committed ourselves to

Christ and to our relationship, and we've never left that love for God or for each other—even after fifty years of marriage.

If you have ever been engaged to be married, you know what it is like to be utterly devoted to someone. Vonette and I were separated by many miles, she in Texas and I in California, but I kept a constant stream of special delivery letters, flowers, candy, and long-distance phone calls flowing in her direction. I did everything I could possibly think of to impress and woo her, because I wanted her to see how serious I was. I wanted her to feel the same way about me as I felt about her. Romantic love surprises us as it brings out creativity we never knew we had. And there is a deep longing as well; I can remember eagerly anticipating the time when we could actually be united in marriage, never to be separated.

I was experiencing these same feelings toward God. I wanted *Him* to be with me for the rest of my life, too. I did everything I could to please Him, and devoted much time to prayer and the study of His Word. I spent five years at Princeton and Fuller Theological Seminaries because I desired to learn more about Jesus. I yearned to know Him better and to be drawn closer to His great, loving heart, just as I yearned to spend time with Vonette.

Over the years, we have worked hard to make our marriage the best it can be. There have been many occasions when I had to travel for extended periods, and Vonette could not accompany me. I had to work that much harder to maintain the intimacy we had cultivated. Distance and time could easily have become obstacles, but it was a matter of priorities for us to keep anything from damaging the closeness we desired.

There have also been times when I have been irritable or insensitive to my wife. Early in our relationship, as the president of our college/young adult group at the First Presbyterian Church, I was called to counsel someone experiencing a crisis that could have caused great heartache and even scandal to a famous Christian family—even worse, to the family of God. The situation arose suddenly, and I had no opportunity to tell Vonette where I was. I left her sitting for hours after church in a hot car with no clue as to my whereabouts. I could have gotten a message to her, of course, if I had stopped to be more considerate. When I finally returned, Vonette, needless to say, was less than pleased! She felt that if the shoe had been on the other foot, I would have been upset with her. And she was right.

We had to talk that one out. As a matter of fact, we took some time at that early juncture in our marriage to reassess our relationship and our priorities. I discovered that, in many ways, I needed to be more loving and considerate toward her feelings. I needed to make it a habit of apologizing when I failed her, acknowledging my wrongs, and working to change my ways. That is exactly what I did. Good things came out of that misunderstanding and, as a result, I grew a bit in maturity as a husband. Growth is painful! But we have both learned a lot over the years. By really working at it, we have been able to maintain and then *deepen* the love that first drew us together. (Just a simple suggestion to help ensure a happy marriage when problems arise: always be quick to say, "I am sorry. I was wrong. Please forgive me. I love you.")

That has been our life: pleasing Him by loving each other, and pleasing each other by loving Him. It is the most complete joy we know.

I believe our love for God works under many of the same dynamics as a good marriage. Meeting

God for the first time is euphoric. There is a "honeymoon period" of faith in which loving God comes so easily and so naturally. With every new morning we are eager to meet with Him in prayer and to study His Word. We're aware of His presence wherever we go. But over the long years that follow, too often the thrill fades. The initial joy slowly dissipates—until, without being aware of it, we discover that we have left our first love. Young, immature euphoria needs to deepen into something far greater, far more rewarding to us and honoring to God. When we sometimes fail Him, we must confess our sin, repent, and correct our ways.

In doing so we ultimately build a deep, abiding intimacy. Joy is still there, but we become more focused on loving God by serving Him. We find that we experience our Lord most deeply and we please Him most fully when we're doing the things He wants us to do. Vonette and I love to please each other, and we love to serve God together. After half a century, that has been our life: pleasing Him by loving each other, and pleasing each other by loving Him. It is the most complete joy we know.

Recently, while visiting at the home of dear friends, Pearl and Jack Galpin, we read these words from a lovely plaque: "Lord, help me to see thee more clearly, love thee more dearly, follow thee more nearly." These words have become our earnest prayer.

But we are also ever mindful that it is easy to go astray, to lose our moorings and drift away from our first love. At some point, it happens to most of us.

Remember When?

When we feel spiritually dry and empty, and God's voice seems to have been silent for a great period, it helps us to turn to our memories. Memories of God's past goodness are crucial and irreplaceable. Throughout His Word, God calls His people to cling to their history and draw strength from it.

The New International Version says, "Remember the height from which you have fallen!" (Revelation 2:5a). As we remember what our first love was like, we gain perspective—we come to understand the height from which we have fallen. That, my friend, will engage the emotions—our heart. We will feel deep remorse, or what Pauls calls "godly sorrow." After sending a letter of rebuke to the Corinthians, Paul wrote:

Now I am happy, not because you were made sorry, but because your sorrow led you to repentance. For you became sorrowful as God intended and so were not harmed in any way by us. Godly sorrow brings repentance that leads to salvation and leaves no regret, but worldly sorrow brings death (2 Corinthians 7:9,10, NIV).

When you hurt deeply as you realize that the love has gone out of your faith, that is godly sorrow. The right kind of sorrow is a "good pain" because it leads us to repentance. This is when joy occurs.

I must point out, of course, that those who have never known God will have no such memories. If you have never received our Lord Jesus Christ and walked with Him, you cannot know the beauty and grace of that marvelous experience. You will feel a longing instead. You will have an awareness of your failures and limitations as a human being. If so, God's Spirit is beckoning to you, drawing you to Himself. If you are experiencing a deep desire in your heart to turn from your *sins*, as we call our spiritual failures, and to experience God's wonderful love and forgiveness for the first time, be assured that He is waiting for you with open arms. Please read "How to Know God Personally" in the back of this book. It will give the information and help for which you are looking.

But if sometime in the past, you have known God intimately and have presently lost the intensity of your passion for Him, you can be sure that He is waiting for you to return. In the worst of times, when we cannot seem to hear His voice or feel His touch, we still have an amazing resource. We can consult those incredible filing cabinets in the human mind—our memories. Think about something you have enjoyed over the years: Christmas, Thanksgiving, Easter, springtime, football season, vacation in a very special place. When you take the time to relive your memories of these things, your spirit seems to catch a second wind. You feel your excitement begin to build. It is not difficult to develop a frame of mind that feels like a cool, refreshing wind.

Again, I think of how that works in marriage. I return to this example again and again, and there is a logical reason for doing so. Jesus calls the Church —you and me—His *bride* frequently in His Word. The joy of a perfect marriage, great as it may be, is only a dim reflection of the deepest and most intense pleasure of all: knowing God in an intimate, loving, personal way.

Vonette and I find that when we relive our first love for each other, we enhance the memory of those early sparks. We talk over the long ago days when I courted her through the mail; when we had the unique enjoyment of talking about things for the first time, each of us learning how the other thought and felt. We try to recapture some of the eagerness, creativity, and playfulness of those times, and it is amazing how our love is rejuvenated.

Just recently we had two of our grandchildren, Kellor and Noel, visiting us in our Orlando home. Vonette and I enjoyed watching them play a game of Dominoes. After they returned home, I challenged Vonette to a game. We had not played Dominoes for many years. I must say, we enjoyed our time together in this way with much laughter and fun.

Frankly, that happens too seldom with our loved ones and with our Lord. We fall into ruts of stale habits. Ruts are those dusty, well-worn ditches that have been described as "coffins with the ends knocked out." We dare not let our relationships grow stale and dusty. We need that special spark of newness and refreshment, and a wonderful way to find it is by reliving the better times we have shared.

We need to stop and remember—and relive.

Strolling Down Memory Lane

How can you remember the height from which you have fallen when it comes to your relationship with God?

Begin by simply taking the time to reflect. Call on all the resources of your memory and try to recapture a mental snapshot of what that first love was like. Where and when did you first meet the Lord? How did it feel? What were the first things you did? Make a list of the people who knew you then; ask them what they observed in your expressions, words, and actions.

Think about how God changed your life when you experienced your first love for Him. What habits were a part of your life? How did you conduct your prayer life? What sections of the Bible meant the most to you? I suggest that you take a sheet of paper, draw a line down the middle, and make a simple chart. On the left side, write words or phrases describing your feelings and experiences at the time of your first love. Simple things will do. On the right side, note how that item has changed, if it has.

I believe you will find the evidence of slow erosion—small, seemingly insignificant compromises in your original commitment to God. These may not be obvious, consequential matters. Certainly you may still be serving God faithfully, just as those in Ephesus did. You may have excellent church attendance. You may be reading your Bible daily. But do not be surprised if you find that the marks of your early passion have slowly faded and disappeared, often without your noticing.

Do not be surprised if you find that the marks of your early passion have slowly faded and disappeared, often without your noticing.

Then, after you've reflected on that, I invite you to talk to God about your observations. Even if you do not feel His presence, speak to Him as you would any friend or loved one, for He is closer to you than your own heart. If it will help you to focus your thoughts, go to a private place and speak aloud to God. Let the tears flow if they want to come. Be completely candid with Him; He knows you better than anyone, even yourself.

You may also want to begin a "First Love"

journal and write out your prayers to God every day. It will become a diary of your journey back to His loving arms.

Let me assure you of one thing: God is not hiding from you. If you feel the pain of separation from Him, that is a *good* pain—the unmistakable sign of His presence. I do not like to submit to the dentist's drill any more than I imagine you do, but I've learned some interesting lessons in that chair. The dental surgeon tells me that in the case of a root canal, a cluster of nerves must be removed. While this gives me wonderful relief from an aching tooth, my dentist is highly reluctant to perform the procedure. He knows that the tooth itself will now become dry, no longer nourished daily by the flow of healthy blood. In time, dryness will make the tooth brittle and in danger of breaking (that is why the dentist must "crown" the tooth). A living tooth is sensitive; the pain tells you it is alive. A dead tooth simply dries out and gives off no signals.

As long as you feel an ache in your spirit, you know there is healthy life there. God is near—the discomfort is His way of telling you that your relationship needs special care. You may feel dry, but it is not the dryness of death—it is a yearning for life. You may feel pain, but you can know that your pain is fully shared by your Creator, God, and Savior. For every tear you shed, He sheds one along with you. He longs for you to draw closer and feel His comfort. His love, as we've seen, is the greatest and most profound thing in the universe. He is drawing you back to your first love for Him.

Sometimes it is necessary to move through a period of sorrow to reach the destination of joy. As remembrance brings you to remorse, you are ready for the next step. Take heart—the best is yet to come!

four

REPENTANCE:
Removing the Obstacles

Turn back to me again.
REVELATION 2:5B

THE TELEVISION PROGRAM *Dateline* ran a heart-breaking story recently. Fortunately it did have a happy ending. The show reported on a very young Canadian girl named Erika, no more than two years old. On the frigid evening of February 24, 2001, she was sleeping beside her mother. But she climbed out of the bed, wandered out the front door, and spent a freezing night outdoors, unprotected.

When her mother found her, the girl appeared to be frozen. Her legs and body were stiff and there were no signs of life. The frantic mother thought her daughter was dead, but she rushed her to the hospital. There, by the grace of God, the skilled medical personnel worked a miracle and revived Erika. Today there is no sign of brain damage or any other permanent result of her terrible night in the cold. She laughs and plays with other children, carrying no memory of her time in the frigid valley of the shadow of death.

As I think of Erika, I think of John's words again: *Remember the height from which you have fallen!* At one time, we have basked in the warm, safe, and secure presence of our Father. But with the ignorance of children, we have strayed from

With the ignorance of children, we have strayed from His warm, loving arms and wandered farther and farther away.

His warm, loving arms and wandered farther and farther away. Finally comes the time when we find ourselves out in the cold. We need to be in God's arms again; we need to know His love and warmth. But all we feel is coldness and confusion.

This brings us to the second phrase in Revelation 2:5, *"Turn back to me again"*—repentance. In the Bible, the word "repentance" means a *complete turnaround*—both inside and outside. No looking back. Repentance is a lot more than simply feeling guilty. It means moving beyond guilt to transformation. It means turning from going your own, independent, self-centered way to embracing God's will for your life. You put one foot in front of the other, and go back the way you came. That is the only way back to God. As you make that journey, our Lord will light your path. He promised, "I am the light of the world. If you follow me, you won't be stumbling through the darkness, because you will have the light that leads to life" (John 8:12).

I believe this is the critical point, the defining moment in being restored to our first love which we have left behind. How many of us come to the aching awareness of being self-exiled from our dear Father? Most of us. How many of us really, truly repent, redirect, and return? Far fewer, I'm afraid. This could well be the most important chapter in the book for you. I pray that God will take each word and illuminate it specifically for your life and circumstances.

A Breath of Fresh Air

You might be aware that this chapter's topic is particularly close to my heart. For many years I was troubled by the observation that even after receiving Christ, so many people live in various degrees of defeat. Why, I wondered, was there so little love among many believers? And particularly, why did I so often struggle with my own sins and shortcomings? There were occasions when I was inconsiderate and self-centered, even though I knew that the Spirit of God lived within me.

Through the ministry of Campus Crusade for Christ, we had given all of our energies to helping take the gospel to the world—sharing the message of God's love and forgiveness through our Lord Jesus Christ. We were having a great deal of success. But we knew there had to be more than the acceptance of Christ: How could we help new believers maintain their first love for Christ and mature in their faith, love, and fruitfulness for Him?

I came to understand that sin steals back into our lives, even though Jesus has completely conquered it. He has removed the deadly venom from the serpent, Satan. Though defeated at the cross, that snake is still capable of biting if we do not keep our distance. I have seen it so often in my life as well as in the lives of people I know and love. We know Christ but we struggle with sin. Paul spoke of the conflict between the flesh and the Spirit in Galatians 5:16,17:

> *So I say, live by the Spirit, and you will not gratify the desires of the sinful nature. For the sinful nature desires what is contrary to the Spirit, and the Spirit what is contrary to the sinful*

nature. They are in conflict with each other, so that you do not do what you want (NIV).

Many years ago, while grappling with this truth, I experienced a moment of inspiration. God showed me a word picture of *spiritual breathing.* God's loving presence, He helped me to understand, is much like the air we breathe. We cannot live—*truly* live—without it. Believe me, I understand this concept of spiritual breathing more clearly now than ever. Because of my pulmonary fibrosis, I use a tube to help my lungs take in pure oxygen almost 24 hours a day. Every breath is precious. But many years ago, when my physical breathing was taken for granted, I first grasped this concept: we need to watch what comes into our systems.

We dwell in a very polluted world, and we breathe in many unhealthy things every day. Often, by watching television or listening to music, we breathe in foul things from our world's culture. Spending time around certain people who are poor influences, we take in polluted ideas. We need to exhale the pollution of sin, and inhale the goodness of God's forgiveness and grace.

When you sin by committing a deliberate act of disobedience, spiritual breathing restores the fullness of God's Holy Spirit in your life. It is an exercise in faith that enables you to continue to experience God's love and forgiveness in your life. Spiritual breathing is simply exhaling the impure and inhaling the pure. Here is how it works:

- *Exhale:* Confess your sin—agree with God concerning your sin and thank Him for His forgiveness of it, according to 1 John 1:9. Confession involves repentance—a change in attitude and action.

- *Inhale:* Surrender the control of your life to Christ, and appropriate (receive) the fullness of the Holy Spirit by faith. Trust that He now directs and empowers you according to the *command* of Ephesians 5:18 and the *promise* of 1 John 5:14,15.

Ever since the day this idea came so clearly to me, our ministry has taught the concept of spiritual breathing for daily, immediate confession of sin, and for appropriating the fullness of the Holy Spirit by faith as a way of life.

This one concept has enriched my life like no other. I discovered that there was a way for me to take my sins and lay them before God even as I struggled with them. And over the years, I've been told by many other believers that the practice of spiritual breathing has liberated them spiritually. There is nothing special about the concept itself. But our spiritual lungs are choking on foul air, and we do not even realize it. We must remember the height from which we've fallen— up on that spiritual mountaintop, where the air is pure and clean. Then we must take a deep breath of air administered by God's Spirit, and turn back toward the heights we would like to reach once more.

Prayer and Fasting

I would like to commend to you one further discipline. This one is seldom practiced but, like spiritual breathing, fasting will help us recapture our first love.

Over the last twenty-five years I have sensed the need for spiritual revival in our country. The simple, personal principles that we are exploring in this book can also be applied to us as a nation. There can be no disputing that our country has forsaken the first love it had for God two centuries ago. We as a nation need to remember the height from which we have fallen. We need to repent and return to the godliness and devotion that made our nation great in the past. The Bible teaches that just as you and I can consecrate ourselves to our gracious Lord and return to our first love, so an entire country can do the same on a corporate level. That is the reason millions of Americans are praying for revival.

I have come to the conclusion that to confront the deeper spiritual issues—the most stubborn strongholds of sin—we need to embark on a journey of intense prayer and fasting. Before revival can occur in this or any other nation, we need thousands, even millions, of believers fasting, praying, and seeking God's face. Prayer brings us directly into God's presence; fasting heightens our dependence and sensitivity to what He wants to say to us. I always recommend safe and healthy fasting, with distilled water and pure vegetable and fruit juices (no solids), plus vitamins and minerals to meet your body's essential needs.

Fasting and praying have certainly changed me. As I have dedicated myself to fast for forty days at a time each year since 1994, intensely seeking God's face, I have experienced many benefits, especially a greater intimacy with Him. I have experienced His leading with unprecedented clarity.

64

I have written several books on this topic, and our ministry published an entire book of inspiring testimonies about fasting from across the nation. People have experienced personal repentance, spiritual revival, and a fresh vision from God through prayer and fasting. Many of them had previously been aware of the distance they had fallen from their first love for God. But somehow they lacked the true desire to change things in their lives—to exhale the impure influences that had taken hold

To confront the most stubborn strongholds of sin, we need to embark on a journey of intense prayer and fasting.

of them. Through dedicated prayer and disciplined fasting, they were able to repent in a much more profound way. I have many friends across America and the world who point to a forty-day fasting period as their defining moment—the watershed event in which they repented, turned their faces back to God, and once again experienced their first love.

In order to recapture your first love, you will certainly find it necessary to commit yourself more deeply to prayer. If the Holy Spirit reveals sins that have become obstructions in your life, and you find that you lack the motivation to change, you may find it necessary to seek the transforming presence of God through fasting. It will "jump start" your process of repentance.

So Near, Yet So Far

Perhaps you have heard the story of a traveler who was on a business trip. As he drove down the main boulevard, he realized he had no idea how to find the convention center for his meeting. Being a humble man, he pulled his car over to the side of the road, rolled down his window, and hailed an elderly man sitting at a bus stop. "Excuse me, sir," he said. "Can you tell me how much farther it is to the convention center?"

The old man smiled and said, "I certainly can. It depends on which route you want to take. In the direction you're heading, it's many thousands of miles. If you turn your car in the opposite direction, however, it's a block and a half."

So near, and yet so far! You may feel many thousands of miles away from God today, but He is as close as a whispered prayer. The Bible tells us that He never removes His eye from us and never sleeps. If you can no longer see Him, it may well be that you're simply facing the wrong way.

Turning back to Him again is called *repentance*, and it is a word many believers are uncomfortable using today. Perhaps they do not like stopping to ask for directions. But if they did, they would find that God is so near—just a 180-degree turn away.

Sometimes it takes a good bit of resolve to make that turn. We become comfortable in our sin. Our lungs become accustomed to bad air. But pollution is deadly; another word for it is poison. Don't you long for the cool, sweet breath of God? You can turn around, retrace your steps, and run into His arms.

Earlier, we talked about making a simple chart of your life now and comparing it with your life back when you were closer to God. I hope you've done that. Pray over the list. Ask God if there are any more items you need to add. Then I suggest you take a red pen and underline the ones that clearly identify sin in your life. The red ink might suggest the blood of Christ, which has already conquered each one of those items; they no longer hold any power to conquer you—not if you surrender them to Christ.

I trust you can identify at least three issues that call for repentance in your life. Probably there will be many more. Offer them to God. Use the eloquence of Psalms 32 and 51 to express to Him the sorrow in your heart. David wrote these moving words during his time of deepest failure. These psalms are the record of his profound sorrow, remorse, and journey back to the joy of God's presence. If God forgave him his terrible sins —adultery, murder, and deceit —is it not reasonable to believe that He will forgive and cleanse you?

If God forgave David his terrible sins, is it not reasonable to believe that He will forgive and cleanse you?

With your "turnaround" list in hand, pray over each line of these psalms and apply these expressions of King David to your life. Believe me when I say that if you do this, you have reached the turning point in recovering your first love for God:

> *Purify me from my sins, and I will be clean;*
> *wash me, and I will be whiter than snow.*
> *Oh, give me back my joy again;*
> *you have broken me—*
> *now let me rejoice (Psalm 51:7,8).*

Oh, what joy for those
whose rebellion is forgiven,
whose sin is put out of sight!
Yes, what joy for those
whose record the LORD has cleared of sin,
whose lives are lived in complete honesty!
When I refused to confess my sin,
I was weak and miserable,
and I groaned all day long.

Day and night your hand of discipline
was heavy on me . . .
Finally, I confessed all my sins to you
and stopped trying to hide them.
I said to myself, "I will confess my rebellion
to the LORD." And you forgave me!
All my guilt is gone.
Therefore, let all the godly confess their
rebellion to you while there is time,
that they may not drown in the floodwaters
of judgment (Psalm 32:1–6).

Repentance is a moment of pain. But being unrepentant is a *life* of pain. And beyond the moment of the about-face, there is the eternal joy of God's love. You have pursued God now with your mind, heart, and soul. One thing remains.

five

RESUMPTION:
Rejoining the Path of Obedience

...and work as you did at first.
REVELATION 2:5C

IN 1989, THE UNIVERSITY of Michigan played its conference rival Wisconsin in basketball. It was a close game, and Michigan trailed by a single point with only seconds remaining. That was when Michigan's fine guard Rumeal Robinson stepped to the foul line for two shots.

It was the scenario every player dreams about. Robinson had the opportunity to be a hero; he had the game in his hands. If he simply hit one foul shot, he could tie the game and send it into overtime. If he put both shots through the net, his team would have an exciting win.

Robinson missed the first shot. Then he missed the second. Wisconsin's players ran off the course shouting with joy—they had upset the heavily favored Michigan Wolverines. And Rumeal Robinson, the All-American guard, was left standing at the line, hanging his head. He had failed, and in something so simple and fundamental.

Robinson felt great sorrow over that game. He had hit thousands of foul shots over the years, on his way to becoming one of the best shooting guards in college basketball. Growing up, he had stood under the hoop for hours until he could send shot after shot through the net, without even touching the rim. Why had he missed these two?

Some athletes never recover from the failure of a big game, but Robinson put his disappointment into action. He showed up at the next practice, played hard, then remained on the court afterward to shoot one hundred foul shots all by himself. For the rest of the season, that was his daily regimen—one hundred extra foul shots after every practice.

The day came, at the end of that season, when Rumeal Robinson found himself standing at the foul line again. This time there were three seconds remaining in overtime in the national championship game against Seton Hall. Both shots fell easily through the net. Michigan won the NCAA crown.

Today, few remember Robinson's two missed

shots against Wisconsin early in the season. But every Wolverine fan remembers the two graceful ones that brought home the championship. It all happened because Rumeal Robinson felt his failure deeply enough to return to the fundamentals —the things he did when he first loved basketball.

Back to the Basics

When we see how far we have fallen, we are devastated by remorse—the mind engages the heart, and the heart engages the soul. It only remains, as we will see, for the hands to play their part. As Rumeal Robinson understood, sorrow is worthwhile only if it leads us to take action. This is the third directive: "Work as you did at first," Jesus instructs the Ephesians (Revelation 2:5c). In other words, *go back to the basics.*

Notice that He does not say this to a lazy, inactive group of people. The first thing Jesus mentioned was their vigorous activity. "I have seen your hard work and your patient endurance," He told them (Revelation 2:2). But their work had become empty. It had become like a loveless marriage, with all the routine but none of the romance.

I believe this point confuses many believers.

It seems to them that they are serving God with energy and faithfulness, and so they are—just like Martha. What they have failed to confront is the issue of first love, because they are so busy doing all the right things. They go to church. They read their Bibles. They offer a cup of cold water. Isn't that the same as love? Didn't Jesus identify love with obedience? The answer is yes. We *do* serve our Lord because we love Him—we have simply left the joy and the intimacy of Christ Himself. We have become so busy with our daily tasks that we have neglected to sit at His feet.

We do serve our Lord because we love Him—we have simply left the joy and the intimacy of Christ Himself.

In struggling marriages, both spouses tend to insist that they do still love each other. They continue to go through the motions and keep the marriage together. They do all the right things, even giving each other gifts at Christmas and birthdays. What they've left behind is the joy and the intimacy. When that happens, service can no longer bring pleasure. Jesus wants us to see that. He would have us shift our focus from the lifeless things we're doing now to the loving things we did in the beginning. Always remember, living for Jesus is not only what we do for Him but, more importantly, what He does in and through us as we surrender ourselves to Him in response to His love. "We love because he first loved us" (1 John 4:19, NIV).

That is why, at this point in your journey, it is important to "work as you did at first." When your heart has changed toward God, and you have repented of the sin you discovered in your life, you are going to catch a second wind for serving Him. You will serve Him with new joy and dedication. You will go back to the basics.

Now we will explore what those basics might be.

The Second Time Around

The story is told of a man who was immersed in his newspaper one morning as he ate breakfast. Over the paper came the voice of his wife: "I bet you don't remember what today is."

Several alarms went off in the husband's head. "Of course I do, honey!" he said with a romantic kiss. Then he rushed out the door, hurried to his office, and picked up the telephone. Two dozen roses were delivered to his wife—and right behind them, a gigantic box of candy. Finally, near the end of the day, a long limousine pulled up to the front door. The wife was speechless. Her husband helped her into the limousine with a big smile. On the way to the best restaurant in town, he said to his wife, "You see? I *do* remember the significance of today, don't I?"

"You certainly do," smiled his wife. "This has to be the most wonderful Groundhog Day I've ever spent!"

While that fellow may not have possessed the world's best sense of timing, he did understand something about getting back to the basics. He knew how to get to work in a relationship. I would assume that in the early days of their courting, this man did similar things—perhaps with a better feel for the occasion.

When we leave our first love, many things come between our Lord and ourselves, just as surely as that fellow's newspaper was blocking the view. When we feel the deep sorrow of repentance and experience God's forgiveness and love, we want to do the things we once did. Some of these will be obvious—prayer and time in the Word, for example. Other activities for Him will take some thought and prompting by the Spirit.

When you first met Christ, you probably talked to Him frequently. How is your prayer life today? Has it become rigid and routine? Perhaps it would help to find a new place and a new approach for spending time with God. As mentioned earlier, it is a great idea to keep a prayer journal. Pour out your thoughts and your requests to God. Read the psalms and record your personal responses to them. As God works in your life, write down your new thoughts and experiences. You will be able to return to these entries later and praise God anew, as more difficult events occur in your life. The more you know about someone, the more you have to talk about.

I also recommend some fresh approaches to your study of God's holy, inspired Word. Please do not think you can rediscover your first love for God without immersing yourself in His Book. That is the place where we feel the Spirit's touch most powerfully. That is where His great teachings for us are recorded. The words will seem to jump off the pages and galvanize your life. Begin a new, exciting study of the Bible—a cover-to-cover reading or a focus on the Gospels, for example. Go to a Christian bookstore and look for a volume that will jump-start your devotional times.

Once again, think of the things you first did —the "flowers and candy" of your early times with God. How did you practice His presence in your daily life back then? How did you talk to others about Him? What were your relationships like? Review the chart you made earlier to help you get back to the basics.

My friends, it is true that a fresh new joy drives our actions. But it works the other way, too. If you have seen the "fact, faith, and feeling" train in the *Four Spiritual Laws* booklet, you understand that feelings are simply the result of faith and obedience. In other words, do not wait to feel something in order to do something. Know that you can *act* your way into *feeling* much more effectively than you can feel your way into acting. Go share your faith in Christ with someone, whether you feel like it or not. Simply breathe spiritually and ask God to lead you to someone who needs Him. Serve God in a new way. Go downtown and volunteer for a mission project for the poor, and see if that does not energize your love for God. Spend time teaching children or teenagers at your church about our Lord. Encourage a struggling friend. I guarantee you, the feelings will come naturally from your attention to the things God cares

78

about. Ask God to break your heart with the things that grieve Him.

Also, do things that will require you to walk in faith. Sometimes we have lost our feel for God's Spirit because we are not doing anything in life that absolutely requires His presence and power. I challenge you to "put God on the spot" today. After you have confessed all known sin and have the assurance that you are filled with the Holy Spirit (see "The Spirit-Filled Life" in the back of this book), ask Him to lead you to one nonbeliever who needs to hear the good news of Jesus Christ. Ask Him to put you right in the middle of a situation in which you can be His agent. See how real He will become in your life as you depend on Him to do something supernatural.

> *Sometimes we have lost our feel for God's Spirit because we are not doing anything that requires His presence and power.*

When you leave something behind, you retrace your steps back to the place where you left it. Return to the basics—I predict you will find your Lord there, right where you left Him. He is waiting for you.

Loving by Faith

One of the greatest lessons I have learned in my marvelous adventure with Christ is *how to love by faith*. And I learned that life-changing truth during one of the most difficult periods of my life.

One early morning in 1967, a group of 13 of my beloved fellow staff, whom I had discipled and to whom I had delegated great responsibilities, confronted me with an ultimatum. I was to resign the presidency of Campus Crusade for Christ which Vonette and I had founded in 1951 or they would take over the movement, declaring that the entire staff of several hundred would follow their leadership.

After they gave me the ultimatum, that very night God awakened me at 2 a.m. with a message. I had learned to walk closely to our Lord and always sought to listen carefully to any impression I may receive from Him. I tried to live according to the promise of Philippians 2:13: "It is God who works in you to will and to act according to his good purpose" (NIV). In other words, whatever God tells you to do, He will give you the power to do if you love, trust, and obey Him.

In obedience to His leading, I got out of bed, took my Bible and went into another room. I knelt before God with the prayer, "Lord, do you have something to say to me?" For the next two hours, He showed me not only the importance of loving those who had rejected my leadership, but also *how* to love them.

Though His message from His Word was far more detailed, the distilled essence of what God said to me was very simple. It involved two very important words: *command* and *promise*. As believers, we are commanded to love God with all of our heart, soul, mind, and strength, and to love our neighbors as ourselves (Luke 10:27). We are commanded to love our fellow believers (John 13:34,35) and even our enemies (Matthew 5:44).

We know that it is His will that we love Him and others, because that is His *command*. So, by faith, we can ask God to help us love others according to His *promise* in 1 John 5:14,15: "This is the confidence we have in approaching God: that if we ask anything according to his will, he hears us. And if we know that he hears us—whatever we ask—we know that we have what we asked of him" (NIV).

That night, I determined, with God's help, to love each of these men who had been unfaithful to my trust, whatever happened. As a result, I continued to love them then, and still do to this day. God never allowed me to defend myself. In fact, He fought for me. While only six of these key men ultimately left the ministry, the Lord of the harvest sent over 700 new full-time staff to join us that very summer.

Some months later the leader of the coup returned to ask my forgiveness. He explained that the phenomenal success they were experiencing across the country had led them to think more highly of themselves than they had reason to think. "We were on an ego trip," he confessed. We were wrong. Please forgive us."

By faith based on His command and promise, you can love God with all your heart, soul, mind, and strength.

You love others in the same way you love God. You obey His *command* to love Him and others, and you claim His *promise* that if you ask anything according to His will, He will hear and answer. By faith based on His command and promise, you can love God with all your heart, soul, mind, and strength.

six

REVIVAL:
Rejoicing in the Light

God will rejoice over you as a bridegroom
rejoices over his bride.
ISAIAH 62:5

HE WAS STILL A YOUNG man, but you might not
have guessed it at first glance. In the space of a
few months, his youthful vigor had given way to
the pallor of hunger and illness.

He had lived the high life, if only for a season. He had run through a small fortune in cash
without looking back. As long as the money held
out, there were plenty of women, plenty of parties, plenty of good times. But when the last bills
had fallen from his wallet, he was not really surprised to see the "friends" fall away, too. Now he
was alone.

As the young man considered the heights he
had once held, he discovered that high living and
high standards were two separate things. The wild
times and parties were no more than a cruel mi-

rage, but his family and his home now appeared to be a higher place in life than he had realized. Father had cared for all his needs, sparing no expense, but he had taken all that for granted! Fine clothes, servants, a full table—and now he had to scramble for table scraps. Now he was little more than a slave, unfit for the lowest level of servant in the household of his youth. There was no doubt about it—high living had made him a low-life young man.

The thought of it now pierced his heart. He saw for the first time the corruption inside him— the foolish rebellion that had caused him to demand his money and leave. How could he have inflicted so much pain on his father for the price of a sack of coins? His eyes flooded with tears. There he sat, muddy, slumped against a trash bin in the worst part of town, weeping uncontrollably. The other beggars thought he was intoxicated, but he was filled with only remorse and homesickness.

The young man stood up and turned around, facing home with eyes and soul. He would make the long journey somehow, in the hope that he would be taken in and allowed to tend the pigs. It was the worst job he could think of, but it did not matter—anything to be home again; anything to see his father. But how would he be received? Had his father disowned him?

After a long journey, he was slowly approaching the old familiar place at sunset. Squinting his eyes to see the estate, he caught sight of a dim figure by the side of the road. It was just an outline, a thin silhouette, yet the body language was unmistakable. The figure strained forward, as if studying the intersection of the road and the horizon—*his* direction. The figure rose tentatively, then broke into a sprint up the road. It was the awkward gait of an older man who has not moved so quickly in years.

It was then that the young man knew—his father would meet him more than halfway. His homesickness was nothing compared to the grief his father had experienced over his absence. Tonight there would be a party—*such* a party! Its light would cast out the darkness of his wickedness, and its joy would erase the emptiness of squandered opportunities.

Let the Celebration Begin

The familiar tale of the Prodigal Son (from Luke 15:11–32) is one more story of returning to the love of God once it has been left. The young man wandered from his father; he fell from the nobility of his birthright. Then, in true Revelation 2 form, he considered the height from which he had fallen. He repented and turned his face toward home. Only the details are different from those of your life or mine. But the most striking element of that story, in my opinion, is not its depiction of the son's sorrow. The greatest truth is seen in its dazzling portrait of our Father's forgiveness. He waits patiently for the son to return, and greets him with precisely the opposite of the reaction we might expect.

With this father there is no bitterness or re-crimination. There is absolutely no thought of demanding that the son earn his way back into his father's graces, as the son is more than ready to do.

> *"While he was still a long distance away, his father saw him coming. Filled with love and compassion, he ran to his son, embraced him, and kissed him" (v. 20).*

No matter how long I live, I will always be deeply moved by that verse. It tells me all I need to know about the loving heart of my Lord.

Is your image of God consistent with the portrait in Luke 15? Jesus wants us to see that God is like this father who is wildly joyful, overflowing with love and compassion, embracing and kissing a son who surely smells of filthy hogs, a dusty journey, and a sordid life. Neither the rags, the smell, nor the wrongs of the past mean anything at all to this father—only the heart that turned toward home.

Consider this: If you and I could indelibly etch such a picture of God into our hearts and minds, how might it affect our love for Him? How much easier would it be to maintain our first love?

I think too many of us have the opposite idea of God. We imagine Him glowering at us behind the fortress walls of heaven, scowling as we pound on the door. We know we've sinned, and we're afraid of the inevitable confrontation with His anger and derision. We imagine Him sitting within those walls smoldering with wrath, measuring out eternity in punishments to answer our rebellion. With that tragically inaccurate understanding, it is no wonder many people are afraid to turn *or* return to Him.

Yes, God does hate the cheap sins and false gods for which we desert Him. He *does* have wrath, and He does judge sin. But He looks upon His stray children with love and compassion. He waits with His eyes on the horizon, day after day. Then —before we can even return to Him—He meets us halfway, heaping blessings upon blessings on our head, declaring a celebration in heaven. Remember the father in Luke 15. He killed the finest calf, the best he had, the one he was saving for the ultimate celebration.

That is how God feels the moment you take one sorrowful, halting step in His direction. As His joy overflows, He bestows the deepest blessings, the good things He has been storing away for you. His joy cannot be contained. It has been said that when we take one step toward God, He takes more steps toward us than there are sands on the beaches of the world.

Earlier in Luke 15, Jesus describes how God comes after us. He tells the story of a shepherd who leaves his great flock of sheep to find the lost one. Jesus says in closing the story:

> *"There will be more rejoicing in heaven over one sinner who repents than over ninety-nine righteous persons who need no repentance" (v. 7, NIV).*

That is what I want most for you to see in this chapter: the overwhelming joy of God over your return to your first love. When you have been reunited with the Good Shepherd, your joy cannot even compare to the boundless delight He feels.

Isn't that a wonderful thing to know?

"God will rejoice over you as a bridegroom rejoices over his bride" (Isaiah 62:5).

That is how God feels about you right this moment, as you read these words.

Life in the Light

When we repent and return to our first love, we will experience the joy we long for—a revival of our spirit. In David's moving prayer of repentance, he prayed:

Create in me a pure heart, O God, and renew a steadfast spirit within me...Restore to me the joy of your salvation and grant me a willing spirit, to sustain me (Psalm 51:10,12, NIV).

How will your life change when you've rediscovered your first love? I feel there are three changes that will take place in your life.

First, your intimacy with God will grow to become deeper, more profound, and more rewarding. Some of those unworthy ideas about God—that He is always frowning, shaking His head and grumbling as He looks at you, for instance—will fade away in the light of His genuine nature. You will bask in the true warmth of His love, grace, and compassion.

So transforming, so gratifying will that experience be that you will not be able to leave His side after you return to your first love. Instead, you will practice His presence wherever you go. Yes, you will abide in prayer for richer, more generous portions of your day not because you have to, but because you want to. That time of fellowship will continue between you and God throughout your day, whatever you may be involved in doing, as you experience the reality of His presence as a way of life.

As a result, you will see your life and experiences through new eyes. You will avoid poor decisions and temptations that might have tripped you up in the past. You will abide with Christ, and He will abide with you. And as this happens, He will be slowly sculpting you into His image. In time, you will be an entirely new person—one who bears a greater resemblance to your Lord, and one who bears a lesser resemblance to the old self, the one who lived selfishly and in rebellion. And wonderful fruit will spring up in your life, for your ministry in the world will be greatly enhanced.

That last part, of course, brings us to the second change in your life. You will begin to have a significant impact on other people. Your relationships will be far more dynamic than they have ever been. John wrote, "If we are living in the light of God's presence, just as Christ is, then we have fellowship with each other, and the blood of Jesus, his Son, cleanses us from every sin" (1 John 1:7). That first chapter was one of the first I memorized when I became a believer in Christ. These truths had a powerful impact on my life. I realized that loving God leads to loving people, because Christ died for them. That is why Vonette and I responded to Christ's call to help fulfill His Great Commission in our generation.

I realized that loving God leads to loving people, because Christ died for them.

You will have a greater compassion toward others, and others will be more attracted to you as well. A friend once asked Charles Wesley why people were drawn magnetically to him every-where he went. Wesley replied, "When you set yourself on fire, people just love to come and watch you burn." Those around you will see the spiritual fire, the "first love," within you, and they will be motivated and inspired by your example. You will not be able to resist sharing the fire—but even if you did not say a word, you would find yourself drawn into conversations about Jesus. A city on a hill cannot be hidden. You will stand out in your world, and people will have questions about the burning passion in your eyes and your work. Your greatest joy in life will come from help-ing other people to find the same joy you have found in knowing, loving, trusting, and obeying our dear Lord.

If you are married, your marital relationship, too, will be enhanced by your first love for God. You will learn how to love your spouse sacrificial-ly as Christ loves His bride. If you are a parent, you will care for your family flock in a way that reflects the wisdom of the Good Shepherd. If you have a career, you will relate to your coworkers in a way that sets you apart as His workmanship. As you abide in the presence and love of God, your relationships will never be the same again.

The third and final change in your life will be that God's love will flood your heart with His peace. The world is filled with people in turmoil. Every single one of us was made to live and thrive on the love of our wonderful God. When we try to live in any other way, we can only find ourselves eventually at war within. We become like the Prodigal, picking at scraps in the trash bins of the world when we could be dining at the table of our king. We sense there is more, and we know there must be abundant living somehow. Whether we seek peace through money, fame, possessions, pleasure, or some other cheap substitute, we will find no lasting happiness until the love of God envelops us with His supernatural peace.

Vonette and I do not think of our contract to be slaves of Jesus as a sacrifice—anything but! It is the most liberating action we could ever have taken. Because of our love and our deep gratitude for all He has done for us, we chose to surrender ourselves and all that we possessed or ever would possess to Him, our great God and Savior. As a result we have been spared many worries and anxieties. We have not pursued fame or glory, wealth, praise, or applause of others, but instead we have offered ourselves as His slaves for His glory. We signed our commitment as a fully binding contract and we have approached it seriously, like any other contract, ever since. We have therefore been freed from pettiness, resentment, and competitive internal and external conflicts. We have the freedom and energy to do the things God has called us to do, because we are not fighting a civil war within our souls. Our first love has helped us to maintain our inner peace.

Simply serving God was not enough. I longed to possess a heart overflowing with love and praise for my Lord.

Have you found a peace such as this? Are you experiencing the sweet presence of God every day, everywhere you go under all circumstances? Are you a transforming influence among the people who surround you, rather than conforming to their pattern? The love of God will set you free. It will enable you to experience the abundant life that Jesus promised to all who love, trust, and obey Him.

Turning Homeward

I trust you believe that the words of Jesus' story are true—that the God you seek is Someone who seeks you even more intensely. To experience the full and complete joy of reunion with Him, you need only to have responded in faith and obedience to the suggestions we have discussed in this book:

With your mind, you have remembered the height from which you have fallen. You have reflected deeply upon the joy of God's presence and the pain of being apart from Him.

With your heart, you have experienced remorse over the place where your wandering has brought you. When we truly comprehend the despair and judgment that await us without God, it is natural to feel grief and sorrow.

From your soul, you have repented of the sin that ensnared you and stifled your first love. You have genuinely, sincerely renounced the things that have come between you and God.

With your strength, enabled by the Holy Spirit, you have resumed the things you once did to please God. Just as the Prodigal traveled home, you have emotionally and spiritually turned toward your heavenly home as you have returned to your first love for our great God and Savior.

With your total being, you are now revived; you have returned to your "first love." Your mind, heart, soul, and strength have been renewed. You are now experiencing again the joy of your salvation, which you may not have known for years. Now you love God with every fiber of your being.

As you have embraced the above action, you are already feeling the deep joy of your reunion with God. The party has begun! Now take special time to worship and praise your God, even as He celebrates your return. Consider a full day or more to retreat to a place where you can pray, sing, worship, and reflect upon the goodness of God, and allow His refreshing love to sink into your soul. And do not forget to keep serving Him with your hands.

May I suggest one way you might do that? Tell a friend about the deep, incredible joy you are experiencing. Only one thing would thrill your Father's heart more than the sight of you approaching home after your prodigal journey. That would be the sight of *two* figures: you and a friend whom you have invited to share your first love for our dear Savior.

seven

REWARD:
Resting in the Shade of Eternity

Everyone who is victorious will eat from
the tree of life in the paradise of God.
REVELATION 2:7

IMAGINE SLOWLY AWAKENING, as if from a wonderful, refreshing sleep. It feels as if you're a child again, waking to the first morning of a glorious spring. You are filled with the kind of youthful energy and excitement you have not felt in—well, far too long.

You yawn, stretch, and feel the gentleness of the breeze rippling your hair. The dampness of the dew is beneath your bare feet. It is clear that you are outdoors, though you cannot quite remember why. And the last dream of your slumber seems just beyond your grasp. Where are you?

Well, there is a stone wall that is hard to ignore. It rises sturdily behind you and encircles you. It appears that you are enclosed in a lush, circular garden. Just beyond your feet are flowers—flowers such as you've never seen before, exploding with the color of light at the height of their bloom. They rise gracefully to the crest of a hill at the very center of the garden. And there at the crest, towering majestically into the sky—an amazing tree.

From the moment that tree fills your eyes, you can look upon nothing else. Surely there is no other tree like it on earth—if indeed earth holds this dreamland in which you've found yourself. The great, colossal trunk must be many thousands of years old. The roots must sink to the very core of the world. And the branches must reach somewhere beyond the sky. There are so many of those branches entwining themselves into the clouds that you cannot count them.

Then you see it—the one fruit, hanging from its vine and dancing softly in the breeze.

What kind of fruit is it? Well, it is not an apple—not exactly. It is not a peach or pear. Nor is it any member of the citrus family. It is not a fruit like any you have seen before. Yet somehow you know that it is there for *you*. It is been waiting there, ever ripe, ever sweet, since the day you were born. No doubt, the purpose of your life has been to come to this place and taste this delicious fruit.

Closing your eyes, you taste it eagerly—and suddenly your eyes open to a new world.

Walking Through Walls

This story is a simple retelling of Revelation 2:7, the encouragement Jesus offers to the church at Ephesus: "Everyone who is victorious will eat from the tree of life in the paradise of God."

If you know your Bible well, you have caught the beautiful symmetry of that passage, found on the final pages of the Scriptures. In Genesis, Adam and Eve were placed in a perfect garden. They were able to walk and talk with God, enjoying the deepest fellowship with Him. But one action was forbidden to them: they were not to eat from a certain tree. As we all know, they did it anyway —and they left their first love, their first home, and their first access to God. They left behind their immortality, too. Concerned that Adam and Eve would then eat from the tree of life and remain forever in their spiritual state—separated from God—He evicted them from the garden.

But here in Revelation 2 we find the wonderful conclusion to the story. It turns out that some will eat from that tree of life even yet—with God's full blessing. And they will have full, perfect, and unbroken fellowship with God forever, in a way that even Adam and Eve, in their initial perfection, never experienced. The original Greek language uses, for *paradise*, a word of Persian origin meaning "a garden surrounded by a wall."

How has the wall come to surround the first home of Adam and Eve? It was placed there by sin—theirs and ours. And how are we described in verse 7? As people who are "victorious." Other translations describe us as those who "overcome" or "conquer." Jesus is speaking to those who walk through walls.

And how do we do that? Through the Lord Jesus Christ—the Overcomer, the Conqueror, the Victor. Jesus has finally brought us back to that garden where it all began. And this is the ultimate conclusion of first love—that we recover the perfect relationship with God that mankind left at the beginning of time. We will finally spend our days face to face with the King who planted the garden and set the tree in place, who has waited for all time until the day when you and I would remain with Him forever.

My word skills are limited, but I hope you can appreciate the breathtaking beauty of this scene. We may not taste the delicious juices of that fruit for a little while, but for now we cling to our first love. That love, you see, is our hope. It is our *foretaste* of glory divine. As we taste the love of God, we bloom spiritually in a way that is no less majestic than that tree. Our roots are set in eternity. We lift our hands to the heavens, worshiping the One who tends and waters us. And we produce wonderful fruit in its season.

Without the love of God, of course, life is not majestic at all. There is a dryness, an emptiness about it. Our branches produce only dead leaves. There is decay from the very roots, and we can sense the dust of death. Life without God's love is little but despair and longing. It is not a life worth living.

> *Life without God's love is little but despair and longing. It is not a life worth living.*

I think back now over half a century, since 1945, when I was first awakened to the wonder of His love for me. It seemed then, and seems now, a miracle. I cannot quite think of myself as a tree—it is easier for me to imagine myself as an insignificant little termite somewhere gnawing on the roots. And yet I know that God sees in me the potential He created me to attain one day. He loves me. I know that I've loved Him more fully with each passing year. I know that I am only able to properly love Vonette, our children and grandchildren, our many friends, our brothers and sisters in Christ, and the entire world because He lives within me and loves them through me.

My Lord has blessed me with so much abundance, so much love, so many thrilling plans worth pursuing, that I find it impossible at 80 to adapt to retirement and to "slow down." I love the life He has given me in this world. And yet I know that the day will come when I will awake without the oxygen tubes on which I now depend. I will feel full strength and vigor in these legs again. I will have the ability to run like the wind. But my only desire, upon awakening, will be to taste of the fruit of the tree of life—to know that I have all of eternity to learn about my Savior and discover God's glorious attributes. "All that I know now is partial and incomplete, but then I will know everything completely, just as God knows me now" (1 Corinthians 13:12).

> *If this love I have now—this first love—is only partial, I can only say that I long for the final edition.*

If this love I have now—this first love—is only partial, I can only say that I long for the final edition. If the abundance of this life is only a foretaste, I long for the full meal. And if my comprehension of God now is just a glance through a hazy mirror, I long for a complete and unimpaired view. Praise God, what a day that will be! I can hardly wait.

But for now, we have something wonderful. It cannot compare to the glories of heaven, but it is still the most wonderful thing in this world. I refer to the indescribable love of God. Cling to it. Cherish it and nurture it every day. Make your first love be your lasting, permanent love, and God will grant you wonderful blessings beyond any imagining. And be sure to share your renewed first love with others.

CONCLUDING PRAYER

IF YOU SINCERELY DESIRE to return to your first love for God, please pray this prayer now and regularly the rest of your life.

> "Father in heaven, I sincerely desire to love you with all of my heart, soul, mind, and strength. And I want to love my family, my neighbors and friends, even my enemies. I realize that I am incapable of loving you and others in my own strength. So, on the authority of your command to love and your promise to hear and answer this prayer, I claim by faith that in the mighty name of Jesus you will answer my prayer."

GROUP DISCUSSION QUESTIONS

1. With Ephesus as an example, discuss how a church can be doing so many things right yet lose their first love.

2. How might this apply to churches today? To your church?

3. How might this be avoided in churches today?

4. How might this apply to individual believers today but not to their churches?

5. List and discuss attractions in this world that may not be sin in themselves but that compete for what should be our first love for God.

6. Discuss how we can have victory over such attractions.

7. Have each member of the group think of a particular attribute of God and explain what it means to them. Other members may add

insights on each attribute mentioned that are meaningful to them.

8. Have each group member mention one way in which our first love for God can be demonstrated. Discuss.

9. Have group members give examples of "unlovable" people they have known. Discuss difficulties in loving them.

10. Allow group members to give examples of how such difficulties were or can be overcome by God's love.

SELF-STUDY GUIDE

1. What was the Lord Jesus' main complaint against the church at Ephesus? (Revelation 2:4)

2. What was His warning to them, if they did not repent? (Revelation 2:5) What does that mean?

3. What, or who, should be our first love? (Matthew 22:37–40)

4. Why is first love important?

5. Why should God be our first love? (Deuteronomy 5:7; Matthew 10:37; 1 John 4:19)

6. Think of seven of God's wonderful attributes, and describe them.

7. How has He demonstrated His attribute of love?

8. What did God do for us that His Law could not do? (Romans 8:3,4)

9. Name four ways we can keep God as our first love.

10. What is a good test to determine if we really love God? (1 John 4:20,21)

11. How important is it to love other people? (1 Corinthians 13; James 2:8)

12. What can we do if someone is not very likable?

13. Write down your understanding of spiritual breathing.

14. Write down your understanding of how to love God and others by faith.

WOULD YOU LIKE TO KNOW GOD PERSONALLY?

The following four principles will help you discover how to know God personally and experience the abundant life He promised.

1 *God loves you and created you to know Him personally.*

God's Love
"God so loved the world that He gave His only begotten Son, that whoever believes in Him should not perish, but have eternal life" (John 3:16).

God's Plan
"Now this is eternal life: that they may know you, the only true God, and Jesus Christ, whom you have sent" (John 17:3).

What prevents us from knowing God personally?

2 *Man is sinful and separated from God, so we cannot know Him personally or experience His love.*

Man Is Sinful

"All have sinned and fall short of the glory of God" (Romans 3:23).

Man was created to have fellowship with God; but, because of his own stubborn self-will, he chose to go his own independent way and fellowship with God was broken. This self-will, characterized by an attitude of active rebellion or passive indifference, is an evidence of what the Bible calls sin.

Man Is Separated

"The wages of sin is death" [spiritual separation from God] (Romans 6:23).

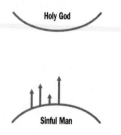

This diagram illustrates that God is holy and man is sinful. A great gulf separates the two. The arrows illustrate that man is continually trying to reach God and establish a personal relationship with Him through his own efforts, such as a good life, philosophy, or religion—but he inevitably fails.

The third principle explains the only way to bridge this gulf...

3 *Jesus Christ is God's **only** provision for man's sin. Through Him alone we can know God personally and experience God's love.*

He Died In Our Place

"God demonstrates His own love toward us, in that while we were yet sinners, Christ died for us" (Romans 5:8).

He Rose From the Dead

"Christ died for our sins...He was buried...He was raised on the third day according to the Scriptures ...He appeared to Peter, then to the twelve. After that He appeared to more than five hundred..." (1 Corinthians 15:3–6).

He Is the Only Way to God

"Jesus said to him, 'I am the way, and the truth, and the life; no one comes to the Father, but through Me'" (John 14:6).

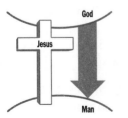

This diagram illustrates that God has bridged the gulf that separates us from Him by sending His Son, Jesus Christ, to die on the cross in our place to pay the penalty for our sins.

It is not enough just to know these three truths...

4 *We must individually **receive** Jesus Christ as Savior and Lord; then we can know God personally and experience His love.*

We Must Receive Christ
"As many as received Him, to them He gave the right to become children of God, even to those who believe in His name" (John 1:12).

We Receive Christ Through Faith
"By grace you have been saved through faith; and that not of yourselves, it is the gift of God; not as a result of works that no one should boast" (Ephesians 2:8,9).

When We Receive Christ, We Experience a New Birth
(Read John 3:1–8.)

We Receive Christ By Personal Invitation
[Christ speaking] "Behold, I stand at the door and knock; if anyone hears My voice and opens the door, I will come in to him" (Revelation 3:20).

Receiving Christ involves turning to God from self (repentance) and trusting Christ to come into our lives to forgive us of our sins and to make us what He wants us to be. Just to agree intellectually that Jesus Christ is the Son of God and that He died on the cross for our sins is not enough. Nor is it enough to have an emotional experience. We receive Jesus Christ by faith, as an act of our will.

These two circles represent two kinds of lives:

Self-Directed Life
S – Self is on the throne
† – Christ is outside the life
● – Interests are directed by self, often resulting in discord and frustration

Christ-Directed Life
† – Christ is in the life and on the throne
S – Self is yielding to Christ
● – Interests are directed by Christ, resulting in harmony with God's plan

Which circle best represents your life?
Which circle would you like to have represent your life?

The following explains how you can receive Christ:

You Can Receive Christ Right Now by Faith Through Prayer
(Prayer is talking with God)

God knows your heart and is not so concerned with your words as He is with the attitude of your heart. The following is a suggested prayer:

> *Lord Jesus, I need You. Thank You for dying on the cross for my sins. I open the door of my life*

*and receive You as my Savior and Lord. Thank
You for forgiving my sins and giving me eternal
life. Take control of the throne of my life. Make
me the kind of person You want me to be.*

Does this prayer express the desire of your heart?

If it does, I invite you to pray this prayer right now,
and Christ will come into your life, as He promised.

How to Know That Christ Is in Your Life

Did you receive Christ into your life? According to
His promise in Revelation 3:20, where is Christ
right now in relation to you? Christ said that He
would come into your life and be your friend so you
can know Him personally. Would He mislead you?
On what authority do you know that God has an-
swered your prayer? (The trustworthiness of God
Himself and His Word.)

The Bible Promises Eternal Life
to All Who Receive Christ

"God has given us eternal life, and this life is in His
Son. He who has the Son has the life; he who does
not have the Son of God does not have the life.
These things I have written to you who believe in
the name of the Son of God, in order that you may
know that you have eternal life" (1 John 5:11–13).

Thank God often that Christ is in your life and that He will never leave you (Hebrews 13:5). You can know on the basis of His promise that Christ lives in you and that you have eternal life from the very moment you invite Him in. He will not deceive you.

An important reminder…

Do Not Depend on Feelings

The promise of God's Word, the Bible—not our feelings—is our authority. The Christian lives by faith (trust) in the trustworthiness of God Himself and His Word. This train diagram illustrates the relationship among *fact* (God and His Word), *faith* (our trust in God and His Word), and *feeling* (the result of our faith and obedience). (Read John 14:21.)

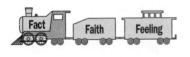

The train will run with or without the caboose. However, it would be useless to attempt to pull the train by the caboose. In the same way, as Christians we do not depend on feelings or emotions, but we place our faith (trust) in the trustworthiness of God and the promises of His Word.

Now That You Have Entered Into a Personal Relationship With Christ

The moment you received Christ by faith, as an act of the will, many things happened, including the following:

- Christ came into your life (Revelation 3:20 and Colossians 1:27).
- Your sins were forgiven (Colossians 1:14).
- You became a child of God (John 1:12).
- You received eternal life (John 5:24).
- You began the great adventure for which God created you (John 10:10; 2 Corinthians 5:17; and 1 Thessalonians 5:18).

Can you think of anything more wonderful that could happen to you than entering into a personal relationship with Christ? Would you like to thank God in prayer right now for what He has done for you? By thanking God, you demonstrate your faith.

To enjoy your new relationship with God...

Suggestions for Christian Growth

Spiritual growth results from trusting Jesus Christ. "The righteous man shall live by faith" (Galatians 3:11). A life of faith will enable you to trust God increasingly with every detail of your life, and to practice the following:

G *Go* to God in prayer daily (John 15:7).

R *Read* God's Word daily (Acts 17:11); begin with the Gospel of John.

O *Obey* God moment by moment (John 14:21).

W *Witness* for Christ by your life and words (Matthew 4:19; John 15:8).

T *Trust* God for every detail of your life (1 Peter 5:7).

H *Holy Spirit*—allow Him to control and empower your daily life and witness (Galatians 5:16,17; Acts 1:8).

THE SPIRIT-FILLED LIFE

Every day can be an exciting adventure for the Christian who knows the reality of being filled with the Holy Spirit and who lives constantly, moment by moment, under His gracious direction.

The Bible tells us that there are three kinds of people:

1. **Natural Man:** One who has not received Christ.

Self-Directed Life

S – Self is on the throne

✝ – Christ is outside the life

● – Interests are directed by self, often resulting in discord and frustration

"A natural man does not accept the things of the Spirit of God; for they are foolishness to him, and he cannot understand them, because they are spiritually appraised" (1 Corinthians 2:14, NASB).

2. **Spiritual Man:** One who is directed and empowered by the Holy Spirit.

Christ-Directed Life

✝ – Christ is in the life and on the throne

S – Self is yielding to Christ

● – Interests are directed by Christ, resulting in harmony with God's plan

"He who is spiritual appraises all things" (1 Corinthians 2:15, NASB).

3. **Carnal Man:** One who has received Christ, but who lives in defeat because he trusts in his own efforts to live the Christian life.

Self-Directed Life

S – Self is on the throne

✝ – Christ dethroned and not allowed to direct the life

● – Interests are directed by self, often resulting in discord and frustration

"I, brethren, could not speak to you as to spiritual people but as to carnal, as to babes in Christ. I fed you with milk and not with solid food; for until now you were not able to receive it, and even now you are still not able; for you are still carnal. For when there are

envy, strife, and divisions among you, are you not carnal and behaving like mere men?" (1 Corinthians 3:1–3).

The following are four principles for living the Spirit-filled life:

1 God has provided for us an abundant and fruitful Christian life.

"Jesus said, 'I have come that they may have life, and that they may have it more abundantly'" (John 10:10, NKJ).

"The fruit of the Spirit is love, joy, peace, patience, kindness, goodness, faithfulness, gentleness, self-control; against such things there is no law" (Galatians 5:22,23).

Read John 15:5 and Acts 1:8.

The following are some personal traits of the spiritual man that result from trusting God:

- Love
- Joy
- Peace
- Patience
- Kindness
- Faithfulness
- Goodness

- Life is Christ-centered
- Empowered by Holy Spirit
- Introduces others to Christ
- Has effective prayer life
- Understands God's Word
- Trusts God
- Obeys God

The degree to which these traits are manifested in the life depends on the extent to which the Christian trusts the Lord with every detail of his life, and on his maturity in Christ. One who is only beginning to understand the ministry of the Holy Spirit should not be discouraged if he is not as fruitful as more mature Christians who have known and experienced this truth for a longer period.

Why is it that most Christians are not experiencing the abundant life?

2 Carnal Christians cannot experience the abundant and fruitful Christian life.

The carnal man trusts in his own efforts to live the Christian life:

- He is either uninformed about, or has forgotten, God's love, forgiveness, and power (Romans 5:8–10; Hebrews 10:1–25; 1 John 1; 2:1–3; 2 Peter 1:9).

- He has an up-and-down spiritual experience.

- He wants to do what is right, but cannot.

- He fails to draw on the power of the Holy Spirit to live the Christian life (1 Corinthians 3:1–3; Romans 7:15–24; 8:7; Galatians 5:16–18).

Some or all of the following traits may characterize the carnal man—the Christian who does not fully trust God:

- Legalistic attitude
- Impure thoughts
- Jealousy
- Guilt
- Worry
- Discouragement
- Critical spirit
- Frustration

- Aimlessness
- Fear
- Ignorance of his spiritual heritage
- Unbelief
- Disobedience
- Loss of love for God and for others
- Poor prayer life
- No desire for Bible study

(The individual who professes to be a Christian but who continues to practice sin should realize that he may not be a Christian at all, according to 1 John 2:3; 3:6–9; and Ephesians 5:5.)

The third truth gives us the only solution to this problem...

3 **Jesus promised the abundant and fruitful life as the result of being filled (directed and empowered) by the Holy Spirit.**

The Spirit-filled life is the Christ-directed life by which Christ lives His life in and through us in the power of the Holy Spirit (John 15).

- One becomes a Christian through the ministry of the Holy Spirit (John 3:1–8.) From the moment of spiritual birth, the Christian is indwelt by the Holy Spirit at all times (John 1:12; Colossians 2:9,10; John 14:16,17).

All Christians are indwelt by the Holy Spirit, but not all Christians are filled (directed, controlled, and empowered) by the Holy Spirit on an ongoing basis.

- The Holy Spirit is the source of the overflowing life (John 7:37–39).

- In His last command before His ascension, Christ promised the power of the Holy Spirit to enable us to be witnesses for Him (Acts 1:1–9).

How, then, can one be filled with the Holy Spirit?

4 **We are filled (directed and empowered) by the Holy Spirit by faith; then we can experience the abundant and fruitful life that Christ promised to each Christian.**

You can appropriate the filling of the Holy Spirit right now if you:

- Sincerely desire to be directed and empowered by the Holy Spirit (Matthew 5:6; John 7:37–39).

- Confess your sins. By faith, thank God that He has forgiven all of your sins—past, present, and future—because Christ died for you (Colossians 2:13–15).

- Present every area of your life to God (Romans 12:1,2).
- By faith claim the fullness of the Holy Spirit, according to:

His command: Be filled with the Spirit. "Do not get drunk on wine, which leads to debauchery. Instead, be filled with the Spirit" (Ephesians 5:18).

His promise: He will always answer when we pray according to His will. "This is the confidence we have in approaching God: that if we ask anything according to his will, he hears us. And if we know that He hears us—whatever we ask—we know that we have what we asked of Him" (1 John 5:14,15).

How to Pray in Faith to be Filled With the Holy Spirit

We are filled with the Holy Spirit by faith alone. However, true prayer is one way of expressing your faith. The following is a suggested prayer:

Dear Father, I need You. I acknowledge that I have been directing my own life and that, as a result, I have sinned against You. I thank You that You have forgiven my sins through Christ's death on the cross for me. I now invite Christ to again take His place on the throne of my life. Fill me with the Holy Spirit as You *commanded* me to be filled, and as You *promised* in Your Word that You would do if I asked in faith. I pray this in the name of Jesus. As an expression of my faith, I now thank You for directing my life and for filling me with the Holy Spirit.

Does this prayer express the desire of your heart? If so, bow in prayer and trust God to fill you with the Holy Spirit right now.

William R. Bright

Founder, Chairman, and President Emeritus,
Campus Crusade for Christ International

From a small beginning in 1951, the organization he began now has a presence in 196 countries in areas representing 99.6% of the world's population. Campus Crusade for Christ has more than 70 ministries and major projects, utilizing more than 25,000 full-time and 500,000 trained volunteer staff. Each ministry is designed to help fulfill the Great Commission, Christ's command to help carry the gospel of God's love and forgiveness in Christ to every person on earth.

Born in Coweta, Oklahoma, on October 19, 1921, Bright graduated with honors from Northeastern State University, and completed five years of graduate study at Princeton and Fuller Theological Seminaries. He holds five honorary doctorates from prestigious institutions and has received numerous other recognitions, including the ECPA Gold Medallion Lifetime Achievement Award (2001), the Golden Angel Award as International Churchman of the Year (1982), and the $1.1 million Templeton Prize for Progress in Religion (1996), which he dedicated to promoting fasting and prayer throughout the world. He has received the first-ever Lifetime Achievement

Award from his alma mater (2001).

Bright has authored more than 100 books, booklets, videos and audio tapes, as well as thousands of articles and pamphlets, some of which have been printed in most major languages and distributed by the millions. Among his books are: *Come Help Change the World, The Secret, The Holy Spirit, A Man Without Equal, A Life Without Equal, The Coming Revival, The Transforming Power of Fasting & Prayer, Red Sky in the Morning* (co-author), *GOD: Discover His Character, Living Supernaturally in Christ*, and the booklet *Have You Heard of the Four Spiritual Laws?* (which has an estimated 2.5 billion circulation).

He has also been responsible for many individual initiatives in ministry, particularly in evangelism. For example, the *JESUS* film, which he conceived and financed through Campus Crusade, has, by latest estimates, been viewed by over 4.6 billion people in 236 nations and provinces.

Bright and his wife, Vonette, who assisted him in founding Campus Crusade for Christ, live in Orlando, Florida. Their two sons, Zac and Brad, and their wives, Terry and Katherine, are also in full-time Christian ministry.